the Publisher, Greenwillow Books, an imprint of HarperCollins Publishers, 195 Broadway, New York, NY 10007. Manufactured in China.

First Edition
19 SCP 13

Library of Congress Cataloging-in-Publication Data

Hoban, Tana.
Construction zone / by Tana Hoban.
p.   cm.
Summary: Photographs illustrate the kinds of equipment and earthmovers found at construction sites.
ISBN 0-688-12284-1 (trade).
ISBN 0-688-12285-X (lib. bdg.)
1. Construction equipment—Juvenile literature.
2. Earthmoving machinery—Juvenile literature.
[1. Construction equipment.
2. Earthmoving machinery.]
I. Title.   TH900.H68
1997   624—dc20
96-5696   CIP   AC

FOR MIELA

RUBBER-TIRED BACKHOE

BULLDOZER

CONCRETE TRUCK

DUMP TRUCK

FORKLIFT CRANE

TAMPER

CHERRY PICKER

CRANE WITH CLAMSHELL BUCKET

CRAWLER BACKHOE

PAVER

ROLLER

FORKLIFT

GARBAGE TRUCK

IN THE CONSTRUCTION ZONE

RUBBER-TIRED BACKHOE

The rubber-tired backhoe digs holes and ditches. Its bucket scoops up the dirt and empties it into a dump truck to be carried away.

DUMP TRUCK

The dump truck hauls and dumps gravel and dirt. A hydraulic ram pushes the back of the truck up, the tailgate opens, and the truck empties its load.

BULLDOZER

The bulldozer moves on crawlers. Its blade pushes away the dirt and grass to prepare an area for construction.

FORKLIFT CRANE

This forklift crane lifts a bag of dry concrete mix, then releases the mix into the funnel of the on-site mixer. Water is added to the mix of sand, gravel, and cement to make concrete.

CONCRETE TRUCK

The concrete truck carries mixed concrete from the plant to the site. The container turns to keep the concrete mixed. Here, the concrete is filling cinder blocks to make a strong building foundation.

TAMPER

The tamper packs down a small area of dirt and gravel. The ground must be hard and flat to support construction.

PAVER

The paver carries hot asphalt in its hopper. As the paver moves, the sides of the hopper come together slowly, forcing out the asphalt. The roller flattens the asphalt to make the surface smooth.

CHERRY PICKER

The cherry picker lifts a worker. The person standing in the bucket can control the movement of the hydraulic arm.

ROLLER

The large roller presses dirt and gravel into a smooth, hard surface that can later be paved.

CRANE WITH CLAMSHELL BUCKET

A crane lowers a clamshell bucket onto gravel. The bucket's jaws open and take a bite of gravel. The crane lifts the bucket, then empties the gravel where it is needed.

FORKLIFT

The forklift picks up wooden pallets holding cinder blocks and tools and moves them around the construction site.

CRAWLER BACKHOE

The large crawler backhoe scoops up and moves gravel and dirt. It digs bigger and deeper holes than the rubber-tired backhoe.

GARBAGE TRUCK

The garbage truck has a hydraulic lift that raises and empties a trash bin into the hopper of the truck. The truck compacts the rubbish, then hauls it away.